MOVING TO MEXICO

RELOCATION AS A RITE OF PASSAGE

SYDNEY METRICK

Apocryphile Press
1700 Shattuck Ave #81
Berkeley, CA 94709
www.apocryphilepress.com

Please join our mailing list at
www.apocryphilepress.com/free
We'll keep you up-to-date on all our new releases, and we'll also send you a
FREE BOOK. Visit us today!

I am dedicating this book to the memory of my teacher and friend, Francis Dreher, a kind and wonderful teacher, therapist and all-around exceptional man.

ACKNOWLEDGMENTS

This book would not have been written without the inspiration, support and encouragement of my friend and editor, Lorrie Nicoles of Tora Writing Services. I'm enormously grateful not only for her ideas, but her ability to add style and zest to my thoughts and words.

Thank you to all those who shared their stories with me. I consider each story a gift.

I extend my gratitude to my husband, Thomas Banks, and my friend, Toni Ryan, for their support and listening, and to Renee Beck, co-author of *The Art of Ritual*. Renee generously and patiently taught me how to be a writer.

FOREWORD

The Baby Boomers, those of us born between 1946 and 1960, began reaching retirement age in 2011 and many took a look at life without work or raising children and started thinking about what would be next. Those in the following group, known as Gen X, may not be at retirement age yet, but they too are starting to look, and plan, for the next phase of their lives.

Changes in finances, health, weather, support systems, and possibilities for the coming years are all considerations. When you're thinking about going someplace you've never been before, you'd typically use a map in some form. You know where you are in life, and possibly have an idea of what you envision as your future. You may have thoughts about what you don't want your retirement to look like, but perhaps have more trouble getting clear about what you do want. As Natasha Bedingfield says in *Unwritten*: "I am unwritten, can't read my mind, I'm undefined. I'm just beginning, the pen's in my hand, ending unplanned."

It took me awhile to turn a vague desire into a plan of

action. I fell in love with Mexico when I visited Zihuatanejo back when I was about 40. Puerto Vallarta was next. I experienced a peacefulness in the countryside that felt like something I'd longed for. Then I had the opportunity to visit the Manzanillo area. I found the ocean and the acres upon acres of coconut palms irresistible. My plan was to find a way to move there within three years – I even talked one of my sisters into going in on a condo with me. But I had no way to finance the move to Mexico and support myself.

At last everything came together. I was in a stable long-term relationship and I was close to being able to receive full retirement benefits. Some rerouting of airline flights, and a friend buying a house outside of Guadalajara in Ajijic provided an opportunity for us to visit an as yet unexplored area. Two days in a village on Lake Chapala and we knew we found home.

Puerto Vallarta •   • Ajijic
Manzanillo •   • Mexico City
       • Zihuatenejo

Moving from one country to another constitutes a rite of passage for many, perhaps even more so for older adults.

Leaving home, friends, family, and all things familiar is a major transition. It all begins with the decision that a change is right, and it's time to make that change. What follows that decision is a process that involves a number of stages.

INTRODUCTION

French anthropologist Arnold van Gennep discussed cultural passages that included rites that signify the importance of life's stages of separation, transition, and incorporation. Rites, or ceremonies, exist for many cultural passages such as births, initiations, marriages and/or funerals. Some of these rituals are religious – such as a Bar Mitzvah – and some secular – like graduation.

Moving to another country is a territorial passage during which you must negotiate the phases of all three: separation, transition, and incorporation.

Separation involves saying goodbye and leaving behind persons, places, or things that have meaning for you, much of which previously contributed to your identity. The ***transition*** is not just about traveling from one place to the next, but rather determining who you are based on who you have been and what you wish to change or expand upon. ***Incorporation*** includes identifying how the person you have been fits—or must be adapted to—your new life, and finding ways to not only be comfortable with any changes but to acknowledge the reality of your new status. For the personal journey, you can think of these steps as: who you are, who you want to be, and how to become that new person.

In real time, this passage may take a week, a month, a year, or more. It will depend on the type of change, the effort you put into it, who you are as an individual, and what resources you have available for support.

The steps we take in planning a life-changing move to another country mirror the five stages of creating a ritual. While the stages are predominantly sequential, they are interrelated. For example, you will likely evaluate as you prepare. You may acquire new information in the execution of your plan that provides more clarity about the intended outcome. The five stages of creating a ritual are[1]:

- Clarifying your intention
- Planning
- Preparation
- Execution
- Evaluation

I've met an extremely wide range of people since we moved from the United States to Mexico. It is true that there are many "gringos" in this area. (For clarity, in Spanish-speaking countries, a gringo is a person – especially an American – who is not Hispanic or Latino.) While many immigrated from various parts of the U.S. and Canada, others were born or lived in countries all over the world. There are single people, unmarried couples, and married couples. Although the immigrant population is predominantly heterosexual, there are many gay couples. And we represent a range of races and cultural backgrounds.

I frequently find the stories of people here fascinating. So much so that I decided to write a book about it.

I've interviewed a diverse group of people who have made the transition from there to here. Every story is unique, and many are exceptional.

Each story addresses the basic stages of planning any transition or ritual:

Clarifying the intention: What was your decision-making process? What was the catalyst to move you into making the decision to move abroad? What let you know that you were ready to make the change and determine the vision for your future?

Planning: What were some of the challenges that you encountered in the process? Did you experience legal, political, economic, and/or physical dilemmas? Were there internal obstacles to overcome in your own thinking and emotions?

Preparation: Can you describe your process for managing the logistics of the move? How did you determine:

- what to sell, what to keep;
- how to physically move yourself, your stuff, your pets;
- where and when to obtain visas;
- where to stay upon arrival, whether to rent or buy;
- what to do about transportation—bring a car, buy a car, no car
- what insurances you need (health, house, car) and how to obtain such

Execution: Was your preparation successful in making the move? Did you feel you were adequately prepared? In terms of your intention, did things unfold as you'd envisioned? Once you arrived, were there additional tasks that required your attention to complete the move?

Evaluation: You made it! In looking back at your process from then to now, what do you wish you'd kept/gotten rid of? What do you wish you knew ahead of time? Are there things you find difficult to adjust to or are simply surprised by? What worked well in your planning process? How do you feel now about your choice to move to another country?

These five stages describe the general process for a "rite of passage." Every individual will go through these in their own distinct way. The following stories illustrate the many ways people can experienced their own "rite of passage" of moving to, and living in, a new country.

CHAPTER 1

WHAT A COINCIDENCE

"The first step towards getting somewhere is to decide that you are not going to stay where you are." —Unknown

PAUL AND LINDA KURTZWEIL

In the first story you'll meet a couple I don't personally know. By coincidence I subscribe to "Two Expats Mexico," a blog with excellent Spanish lessons and information about living in Mexico, written by Paul Kurtzweil. His website, qroo.us, is also information-packed.

Paul was a deputy sheriff in Florida for 25 years before retiring at the rank of lieutenant in 2015. He and his wife moved to Mexico looking to maximize their retirement income.

In his Nov. 9, 2018 post, *Why we chose to live in Mexico instead of the U.S.*, he tells the story of his move with his wife, Linda.

For over 15 years, Mexico was our favorite vacation destination and we would go there as often as we could. We loved everything about the Riviera Maya and we would often talk about moving there *someday*.

We started thinking that maybe *someday* was now.

I started researching everything I could about living south of the border — especially the cost of living. On paper, it looked like we could make it work, but only if we could eliminate all of our debt in the U.S. and reduce our spending.

We decided to give it a try and we then sold, donated or discarded 99% of our belongings in the U.S. We didn't even want the expense of having to rent a storage shed.

We applied for and were granted resident visas at the Mexican Consulate, packed our belongings into four large suitcases, and flew to Cancun with the intention of trying it for a year.

So, How's It Going?

We've been in Mexico for over three years now and we absolutely love it.

We ended up using the money we had left over from the sale of everything we previously owned to buy a condo in a gated resort community and a car. We now live 100% debt free for the first time in our adult lives.

The lack of debt, combined with the low cost of living in Mexico, has made it easy for us to live very well here. We enjoy a higher quality of life than we did in the U.S. and we have plenty of disposable income to enjoy our retirement to the fullest.

This article may make it sound like we moved to Mexico on a whim and we were just lucky it worked out — but that's not the case at all. We conducted countless hours of research and carefully planned our move to increase our odds of success.[1]

In fact, in a November 26, 2018 post, Paul lists their considerations:

1. Safety and security
2. Population
3. Proximity to an international airport
4. Ease of travel
5. Investment potential
6. Community
7. Access to quality medical care
8. Access to beaches

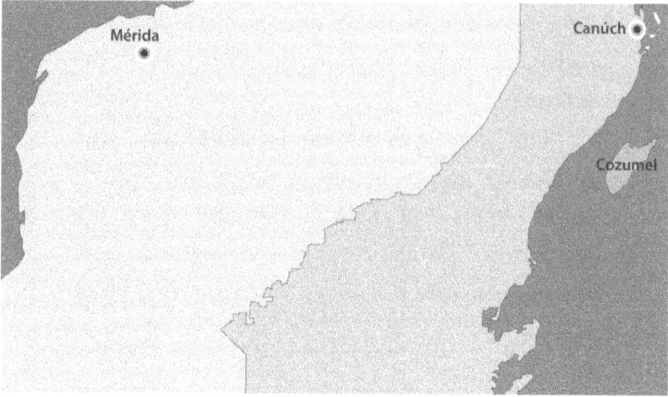

While Paul and Linda have made their home in the Yucatan Peninsula, in the Mexican state of Quintana Roo, the other stories will feature expats all living around Lake Chapala in the state of Jalisco.

WHO ARE THE EXPATS?

A good question, and it is not easily answered.

From a September 30, 2016 article in an *Expats in Mexico* newsletter, I discovered I'm not the only one who has found it difficult to get statistics on expat residency. In fact, it seems the last census was done in 2010. Here's what the article does tell us.

Back in 2010 there were nearly one million foreign-born residents in Mexico. *Expats in Mexico* surveyed readers in 2016 and learned 19% of respondents live in the Lake Chapala area, 13% in Puerto Vallarta, and 10% in San Miguel Allende. At the time those were the top three destinations.[2]

More recent statistics come from the 2017 *Yucatan Times*. Some interesting statistics:

47% of expatriates are women and 53% are men. According to the United States State Department, there are 1.1 million Americans living in Mexico and 1,856,882 expatriates of all nationalities. 20% are between the ages of 23–34, 23% between 35–44. Then there are those that might fit more into the retiree categories—20% of expats fall between the ages of 45–54, and 27% are 55 and above. The Lake Chapala area is the fifth most popular place to settle.[34]

In a 2019 article in *Mexico News Today*, investigative journalist Bill Dahl writes about what he calls a "Mexodus":

According to CBS News, the number of Americans retiring outside the United States is growing exponentially. Between 2010 and 2015 the number grew 17% and the figure is expected to rise during the next ten years as boomer retirement continues.[5]

Lake Chapala, Jalisco, Mexico

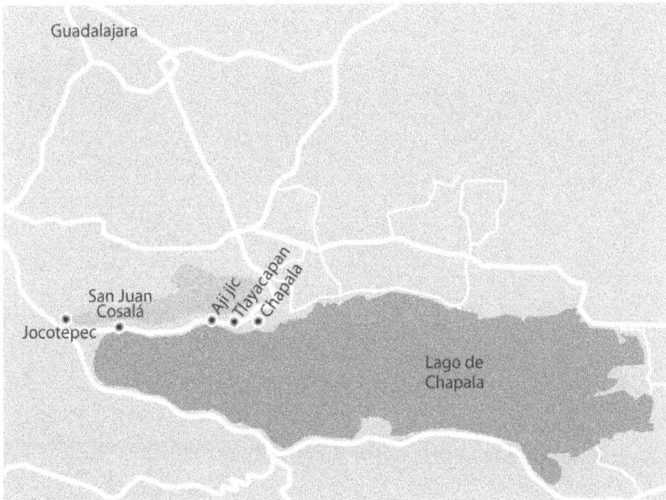

Lake Chapala is the largest freshwater lake in all of Mexico. It spans 50 miles east/west and 7.8 miles north/south. Most expatriates (expats) choose the north shore, known as "Lakeside." From west to east the villages of Jocotepec, San Juan Cosala, Ajijic, San Antonio Tlayaca-pan, and Chapala offer a range of choices for every aspect of living.

Ajijic (Ah he heek) is the most widely known of the villages and the one that has become a destination for many, or a place that just felt like home to others who came through and were converted by its appeal. While "home" may now be here in Mexico for those who shared their stories with me, from there to here was not necessarily a straight journey from point A to point B.

CHAPTER 2

CONTINUING TO WORK IN MEXICO

"If we were meant to stay in one place, we'd have roots instead of feet." —Rachel Wolchin

ISMAT JIVANI

Let me introduce you to Ismat Jivani. Originally from Nairobi, Kenya and the son of parents who died early in his life, he lived with extended family while attending school. Kenya uses the British educational system, meaning that after high school, students either go to trade school or further education to prepare for university. Having been fascinated watching the goings-on in an uncle's bakery, Ismat decided to apprentice as a cook. His applications landed the fifteen-year-old boy a job at a Nairobi Hilton. His five and a half years with the Hilton took him on a journey through North Africa, the Middle East, and Europe.

In 1985 he arrived in Canada — his thirteenth country — and started working as a chef at an upscale French restaurant in Toronto. Five years later, Ismat joined Denison's

Restaurants as a consultant and opened several restaurants for them, and the trend continued. Starting one successful restaurant after another, having married, and fathering three children, he was obviously very accomplished.

So, what led him to find Ajijic? It was a customer with an offer for another consulting job here, opening and running "Number Four Restaurant." Canada had been very good to him; however, competition was taking its toll. Hours were long, Canada was cold, his marriage was over. Since his children were grown, there was nothing holding him there.

The consulting package brought him to Ajijic and gave him a residence and a car for a year. Doing work he loved at a more relaxed pace in a climate more like his native Nairobi, Ajijic felt like home.

While at Number Four, Ismat frequently talked with diners about what foods they missed and craved. He decided to open his own place that catered to people's desires. Thus was born Gossips Kitchen. Shutting down the consulting business, searching for products, and not speaking the language proved challenging, but starting small and serving quality food was a smart decision. Gossips is the favorite of many as a restaurant and for catering. Ismat has certainly integrated fully into the community with his second family — a ten-year relationship and two young boys. He says it's been a long and very difficult journey that he would not do again. Fortunately, all those "there's" have led to a permanent "here" for him and for us.

THOMAS HELLYER

Thomas Hellyer, not quite a baby boomer, tells me he doesn't even recognize the person he was when he moved here in 2008. The move and incorporation into life in Mexico became his entry into adulthood. Here's his story:

While a student at the University of Washington, Thomas thought the best way to keep from failing Spanish was to study the language in Mexico. He began coming to Guadalajara for lessons and would stay until his money ran out. While here, he met and began courting a nineteen-year-old Mexican woman. Together they traveled back and forth to the U.S. over a period of three years.

Thomas's girlfriend, Iliana, enrolled in college in Guadalajara and stayed to study while Thomas went back to Washington to complete his degree in International Business.

Being separated from the woman he loved didn't work for Thomas. He flew back to Guadalajara and asked her to marry him. He needed to go back to the states to begin earning a living, and they aspired to grow a nest egg there. Thomas worked in finance, and over ten years, the couple bought a few properties and had two children. But Iliana missed her family, culture, and the warm climate. Since Thomas was already in love with central Mexico, they decided to make it their home.

Planning a move took some time. When, where, and how needed answers. Guadalajara didn't suit them, but they wanted to remain close to Iliana's family. Research and fact-finding led them to the Lake Chapala area, and in 2007 the decision was made. Finances were a huge problem because Thomas couldn't replicate his U.S. work in Mexico and they didn't have a sufficient nest egg. To make matters worse, when the housing market tanked in 2008, their investments were worth significantly less than before.

Still the move was on. Thomas decided he'd work in real estate and got licensed in Washington as a way to gain knowledge of the fundamentals of real estate. Upon arrival he studied the rules and took the test to join the ranks of local realtors.

Tom and Iliana had magically found an inexpensive rental in Ajijic, where Iliana and the children would live while Thomas went back to Washington to sell their properties.

The actual move was fraught with challenges. With the kids in school they had to move during the summer. Who knew the temperature on the drive could reach 110°? Oh, and the drive...Thomas, Iliana, their two children, and dog caravanned behind Thomas's father, who drove a 24' rented van filled with everything they owned, including appliances. On arriving at the border, they learned that they could not take the van into Mexico and the only place to return the van was four hours away. Luckily, they had a friend with a truck who was able to meet them and ferry their possessions on to Guadalajara. The catch? They had only 24 hours to return the van and reach Guadalajara and collect their things from the friend – who needed his truck empty for work.

The incorporation stage of the Hellyer move was life-changing in more than one way. It was not just Thomas who "became an adult" with the move. Iliana met Thomas at 19, while still living with her family, and then lived in the U.S. for ten years. Coming back to Mexico with two children, to a strange village, with little to no income and no knowledge of how to negotiate the various systems, was overwhelming. She had the good fortune of meeting a nice American couple who took her under their wing and helped her acclimatize during the five months Thomas was back in the states tying up loose ends.

It took a while for them to get acclimated, but now they

are a vital part of the community. In fact, Thomas is a key player in helping others get to "here." Find him out at Chapala Realtors in Ajijic Village. You're also likely to see him driving prospective buyers in any and all neighborhoods. Tom has an encyclopedic knowledge of the area.

"It's very challenging to learn something new as an adult." — *Rashida Jones*

MASANOBU KOYAMI

The percentage of Asians in the area is very low. You can probably fit all those who came from Japan around your dinner table and have space left over. Tokyo-born Masanobu, known to all as Massa, is here, basically, because of the 2011 earthquake off the Northeast Coast of Japan.

In the years prior to that devastating event, Massa worked as a hairdresser in Tokyo. Very adventurous and with a love of traveling, he would go off for months at a time, staying in various nearby countries in Asia and the Mideast, visiting eighteen over a fifteen-year period. Life was good.

Due to a grave traffic accident that required a long rehabilitation, the beauty business was closed to Massa. He transitioned to working as an office secretary, work he continued after the earthquake disaster.

On March 11, 2011, a 9.0 earthquake caused an enormous and savage tsunami. The waves reached up to 128 feet. The tsunami was responsible for a system failure at a nuclear power plant in Fukushima – releasing radioactive material into the environment.

Fukushima was the hometown of Massa's father. The people there lost everything. And then they began to develop various cancers and other diseases. Because the government of Japan had limited resources – and a policy against helping non-Japanese – Massa, along with other volunteers, solicited food, water, clothing, and other necessities for foreigners married to Japanese, and their children, as well as agricultural workers in the Tohoku district. After the tsunami, over a hundred countries pitched in with relief programs, but you can't relieve radiation exposure.

One day Massa's partner Susan said, "We cannot continue living here." He agreed, but where would they go?

San Nicolas de Ibarra, one of the towns on Lake Chapala, is where a friend of Susan's had been living for nearly two decades. Susan had visited many times. Mexico seemed possible. She left Tokyo in 2014 and lived in a number of cities around Mexico. By 2016, Massa was ready to join her. First, he flew to San Francisco for clothes, a bicycle, and a tourist visa. He then cycled to Los Angeles and continued on to Phoenix. From there he and his bicycle flew to Puerto Vallarta, where he got back on the bike and finally made it to Lakeside, where he and Susan both now reside.

With little to live on, Massa decided to use the cooking skills he learned from his mother, who'd been a chef. Selling a range of Asian dishes at the *mercados* held at Sunrise Café in San Antonio Tlayapacan on Mondays and at La Huerta event center on Tuesdays, he soon became part of the community. You can now also find him at Panchos Deli Market in Riberas.

In fact, the community spirit is one of the things he loves about this area. He says everybody helps one another. Massa has every intention of staying, maybe getting a food truck in a few years, and later a restaurant.

WHAT IS WORK?

It's not uncommon to find expatriates, even those of retirement age, who still work in a variety of capacities. Some work virtually, doing the same kind of work they'd done in the past (see the next story); others work on what had previously been "hobbies" but have become sources of income. Many expats work in a wide variety of volunteer capacities. There are so many organizations that provide health care, support, and training. Without listing the many bazars that each support a different non-profit or community, here are just a few of the wonderful groups where you'll find committed volunteers working tirelessly to address community needs:

Escuela Para Ninos Especiales (*School for Special Children*). Their mission is to improve the educational opportunities for children with a wide variety of disabilities and, in doing so, increase the probability that they might enjoy a brighter future.

Hope House. Hope House is a safe shelter for boys ages 8 to 18, helping them develop character, providing love, and imparting tools to be a successful part of society.

Have Hammer Will Travel. Their mission is to provide learning and social experiences within a safe, supportive environment while teaching students basic woodworking skills for exploration of career pathways.

Lakeside Spay and Neuter Ranch & Adoptions, A.C. The Ranch provides shelter and helps curtail the over-population of animals.

Lakeside Youth Philharmonic Orchestra. Golden Strings of Lake Chapala, A.C., trains disadvantaged kids between the ages of 8 and 18 who want to learn a musical instrument, with the possibility of becoming a member of the Orchestra.

La Ola/Casa Hogar, A.C. La Ola Casa Hogar is a children's shelter run as an interfaith children's ministry. Their scope is more than that of an orphanage in that they care for abandoned and abused children as well as orphans.

CHAPTER 3

"RETIRING" TO MEXICO

TOM AND CHRIS

Tom and Chris, a married gay couple, moved here from Austin, Texas in 2017 while both were in their mid-60's. Chris had retired, and Tom worked part-time in a virtual capacity. Both had been exposed to other cultures and were interested in finding a home outside of the U.S.

Growing up in Italy, Chris's parents gave him the sense that they were citizens of the world, thus giving him a life-long openness to other cultures. Tom had wanted to expatriate since adolescence, being intrigued by other cultures and languages. Both are multilingual, so many options were available for their next adventure. As Chris perused the *Live and Invest Overseas* newsletters researching possibilities, Mexico came up as a viable option for several reasons: one, by staying in the Americas, Tom could continue to work remotely; and two, with the lower cost of living there was no need to wait any longer

Their next phase of research was checking out the country to find a good fit. They wanted to live around water, but somewhere other than the coast where the summer heat and humidity are too extreme. After reading a book that focused on moving to Lake Chapala, Chris and Tom came down in November of 2016 to get the lay of the land. They loved the area and the people. Now for the detailed research. After two visits and nearly a month of checking out neighborhoods, shopping, legal issues, safety, access to transportation, and opportunities in the arts, they were ready to act. Chris loved that the area reminded him of his time in Italy as a child. The area is more rural and relaxed. Just what they had in mind.

Their house sold in March of 2017 with a move-out date of June. In April they came down and found a one-year rental within a week. Tom immediately applied for a permanent visa, while Chris went for a tourist visa — allowing them to drive their car down and safely transport their beloved dog, Zelda.

Six months later, they again returned to the U.S., this time to sell the car and get a permanent visa for Chris. By October they found an area that spoke to them, and a home to buy — right up the street from me — and after extensive renovations, moved in May, 2018.

Tom says being fairly fluent in Spanish opened so many doors for them, making the whole moving process much smoother.

After settling in their new home, Tom and Chris say they wish they hadn't brought as much stuff, but otherwise have no regrets. They find themselves surprised by the day-to-day occurrences like cows roaming the street in front of the house, or walking Zelda down the road alongside the arroyo and seeing three horses who'd found their way down to lunch on the greenery. Wanting to integrate into the community, Chris and Tim are disappointed by the overwhelming number of gringos here who seem to create a somewhat divided community based on economic status. Nevertheless, they are determined to create inclusion for themselves in the community at large, as well as in one of their main interests: music. As music has been an important part in both men's lives, they have joined *Los Cantantes del Lago*, a community choir with members from the U.S., Canada, and several other countries. They find joy in performing, and have each reignited a dormant gift — Tom, especially, having been an outstanding vocalist in many performances and experienced in a range of styles from opera through musical theatre. Their passage is nearly full circle.

For many, the incorporation stage is either a return to, expansion of, or exploration of fulfillment. Tom and Chris are like many expats in what may be called "the Third Age." Some think of the years between 65 and 80 as the golden years. According to the Center for Third Age Leadership, the third age equals fulfillment. "Third age begins as advancement becomes less important. Wisdom and self-awareness bring new ease with ourselves and others. Freed from the responsibilities of family and career, we can create our Third Age so it truly becomes a case of 'the best is yet to be.'"[1]

This also aligns with the stages of psychosocial development advanced by psychologist Erik Erikson. Most retirees fit into stages seven (generativity vs. stagnation) and eight (ego integrity vs. despair). Between ages 40 and 65, Erikson suggests, we address the challenges of each stage. "Generativity versus stagnation" describes the need to generate or create things that will outlast us. It's a period of giving back.

Stage eight, called "ego integrity versus despair," begins around 65 and is the last of the psychosocial stages. At this time, we contemplate our life accomplishments and either gain a sense of fulfillment and contentment, or despair, if we feel we've not accomplished our life goals.

From talking with and interviewing those who have come to live Lakeside, I find contentment seems the norm. Perhaps it was present before moving from there to here, but for those who choose to live here contentment seems to increase.

DEE AND TOM GRANT

You don't see many African American couples Lakeside, but you see Dee Grant everywhere. Dee and Tom, like so many others, wanted to leave snowy New York to those who enjoy freezing winters. They'd been boating in the Long Island Sound for forty years and supposed they would retire to a sunny marina somewhere and live on a boat.

But sunny marinas don't prefer full-time residents.

By the early 90's Tom was done working and they began researching possible locations. Their daughter urged them to look into a retirement community in Arkansas, but they truly couldn't see themselves living anywhere in the states. Dee stumbled across *International Living Magazine.* At the time, Portugal and Mexico were highlighted as top localities. Europe seemed so far away, but Mexico...hmmm. More research led Dee to a site that reviewed different cities and towns each month. They'd already traveled to a number of spots within Mexico, and when Chapala came up with a very high rating, they narrowed their focus.

Focus is what ultimately led them to the move Lakeside — the *Focus on Mexico* six-day program, that is. After attending a Focus program in the fall of '09, Tom and Dee made coming back in a year their goal. They rented their house in New York, sold or gave away belongings, and looked for a furnished place Lakeside.

At the time, the *Focus on Mexico* program had "relocation specialists" to assist with any and all questions and needs. Tom and Dee were matched with a woman who helped them find a rental. Four months before the move, Dee quit her job and worked on preparations for the move. Even though they'd made so many contacts in the *Focus* program that facilitated their transition, it was a complicated journey, in part because they drove down and made stops in Virginia, North and South Carolina, and Texas just to say goodbye to family members.

Once here, they then faced the challenge of repeatedly being mistaken as Mexicans driving a car with U.S. plates since, according to Mexican Customs, it's illegal for a permanent resident of Mexico to drive a foreign-plated car.

Upon arriving, settling in was easy. They had already made a number of friends, and Dee immediately got involved in the "meet and greet" program in their condo community. Two years later she was invited to be one of the relocation specialists in the *Focus* program. Even with these commitments, she continues to find time to participate in various performances, organize other events, and generally be a woman about town. Tom, on the other hand, is enjoying the "not doing" typically associated with retirement for the first time in years.

ROD AND LISA STRUSS

Spring in Canada is beautiful, but winter...

Lisa and Rod met while working at a medium security jail in Manitoba. She was head nurse and he was a program facilitator and correctional officer. Their vision was to retire as soon as they could from the jail and, like many snowbirds, find a warm home for the winters. But where to go?

Arizona was warm enough, but neither wanted to live in the United States. Lisa had visited many cities in Mexico over the years, so they began researching options south of the border. A recommendation led them to Ajijic. After visiting so many cities and towns in Mexico, how would they know if Ajijic could be their journey's end? Ajijic had it all. Great weather: check; small town: check; lots of English speakers: check; nice people: check; activities they wanted: check.

Prior to the move they began visiting Lakeside every year for a month at a time. Over a period of eight years, they stayed in several rentals and looked at over fifty houses in the different villages on the north shore.

In the meantime, back in Manitoba...

Lisa had inherited a lakeside cabin from a relative, and when Rod retired, he began the preparations for their move, remodeling the cabin to be their summer home and selling a grain farm that he owned and worked. When Lisa retired it was time to make the move. They wanted a permanent home around Lake Chapala and Lisa started researching online. She found a listing, had a realtor check out the house, made a decision, and sent down a deposit. The house required major remodeling, but they found a contractor who turned a run-down place into an upscale home with a pool.

The visa part of the move was not a big deal because, since they planned to live in Mexico for six months each year, they only needed tourist visas.

But owning a house in another country comes with challenges. Without a temporary (temporal) or permanent (permanente) visa, getting a CURP (Clave Unica de

Registro de Poblacion) — the Mexican version of a U.S Social Security number — is not possible. Without it, forget getting a bank account, electricity, or a driving license. Having a car with Canadian plates, driving back and forth from Mexico (through the U.S.) to Canada each year, and getting the right automobile insurances proves to be an additional and ongoing test of their patience and resourcefulness.

Rod and Lisa have the best of both worlds. They have all they could have asked for and everything they hoped for. Here they have many friends. Rod is a drummer with a band, shoots pool, and works out at a local gym. Lisa rides horses, paints, and spends time with friends. Summers are about driving back to their small town in Manitoba to their four children, siblings, and all that's familiar. This is a great process for people in their 60s. At some point, however, they may choose to — or have to — re-evaluate driving between two countries and two homes each year.

BARB AND DAVE NAISBY

It's a hop, skip, and a jump from the north of England to Inverness Scotland, but over 5,000 miles to Guadalajara. Barb and Dave, born in Sunderland, England, married there, started a dental practice, and begat two children.

At 32, Dave realized he couldn't imagine living in the U.K. for the rest of his life. They looked into moving to Montreal, where Dave's brother lives. However, Dave would have had to spend eighteen months at university to gain Canadian qualifications to continue his practice, and with two young children, this would have been financially impossible.

He still couldn't envisage living and working in his birth

town, Sunderland, until he retired, so Barb and Dave looked into moving to the north of Scotland where they had friends who'd moved from Sunderland. Once the decision was made, it took only three months to sell the house and dental practice and then move north to start their new lives.

But Scotland is dark, cold, and windy four to five months out of a year. Dave says, "Summer in Scotland is the best day of the year." Hence, the question of where they'd go upon retirement. It's common for residents of the countries in the U.K. to move to the Mediterranean, but Dave rejected the Eurozone – not trusting the political and economic stability.

Perhaps somewhere in the Americas would suit? So, they started to consider places like Belize, Panama, and Costa Rica. Barb learned of an exhibition in the U.K. called "A Place in the Sun." She registered and immediately received one of their informational magazines. The first article was on Mexico. While Dave wasn't "straightaway keen" on the country, research revealed Chapala had one of the best climates to be found.

A two-week visit nearly had them convinced, but there was more to learn. They signed up for a six-day *Focus on Mexico* program the next year. The fast-track learning seminars covered a wide range of topics, including health care, immigration, renting, buying, the economy, safety and crime, immigration, and more. Plus, they were able to connect and form relationships with others who'd also be making the move.

Getting information was only a piece of the necessary preparation. They then had to sell their business and house, go to London for visas, and go through the steps needed for Dave to access his pension. With something called QROPS, or Qualified Overseas Pension Scheme, Dave was able to cash in his entire pension at a good exchange rate, so Barb decided to go ahead and buy a house Lakeside.

Golfing and friends from the *Focus* program gave them support and an immediate social network. They say it was easier integrating here than in Scotland, where it can take years to be accepted into a community.

A social network was only one aspect of integrating into the community. Barb spotted a cry for help on a Chapala Web board. Guadalajaran dentist, Miguel Villasenor, was volunteering weekends in the Ajijic Centro de Salud, seeing about 20 patients per day in the free service clinic created to help the poorest people in Ajijic. He needed help.

As Dave was a dentist and Barb a qualified dental nurse, they volunteered. At some point, Miguel needed Barb to do all the administration — making appointments, taking medical histories, and writing up the notes. This was hugely challenging, as she didn't really speak Spanish and Miguel's directions came from behind his mask and impossible to decipher. Between them they developed a dental knowledge base, and it became a joint learning experience. By jumping/being thrown into the deep end, Barb learned to speak Spanish reasonably fluently. Dave, on the other hand, was overwhelmed with being in an environment where he was struggling to understand and insisted on speaking to Miguel in English — helping Miguel enormously with his English skills.

A few years ago, Dave's mother, Audrey, came from England for a visit. When Dave invited her to move, she said, "why not?" and at 85 relocated to an apartment on Barb and Dave's property.

"How do you feel about your choice to move here," I asked the three of them. "This is home," they all agreed.

ANDREA

There are lots of single women Lakeside. Lots. Andrea is one of them. She was born in Germany and spent most of her life in one part of the country or another. However, since childhood she'd wanted to leave the country for some-place that gave her a feeling of belonging. At age twenty she moved to Spain, where she lived for a year and a half and learned Spanish. Family troubles and obligation brought her back to Germany. At the age of 48 she was diagnosed with an autoimmune disease, and four years later, the last of her family had passed on. She cut her final tie to Germany at 61, when her illness began to interfere with work, and she retired.

Luckily, her work for an airline allowed Andrea to feed her wanderlust and explore other countries. She briefly considered Thailand as her destination for retirement. Then, through a German forum she connected with a woman who lived in Riberas del Pilar, one of the Lakeside villages. The woman spoke only German, had a number of physical ailments, and was seeking help and companion-ship. Andrea answered the request. After ten days in Riberas del Pilar, she was ready to leave the less-than-pleasant experience, but not the area. She located a hotel on the lake, stayed three more weeks, and found her peace at Lake Chapala. It became her destination.

The taxi driver who took her to the airport for the trip back to Germany recommended a new condominium complex with rentals in West Ajijic. Back in Germany, Andrea researched and obtained her permanent visa. She sold both of her apartments and all her things and was good to go. With the money from the sales and her pension she was able to purchase one of the West Ajijic condos.

A year and a half later, Andrea decided she wanted a less remote environment and left the condo for a house in San Antonio Tlayacapan. Soon she not only had a house, but health insurance, a car, and a dog.

Now, after nearly four years, she fits right in...almost. She says in many cases she's still a very structured German, very organized, which is a bit of a contradiction to the laid-back frame of mind here in Mexico.

SAM AND GISELE

"Sometimes our lives have to be completely shaken up, changed, and rearranged to relocate us to the place we're meant to be." —Neale Donald Walsch

Sam, born to a Guatemalan father and Salvadoran mother, grew up in El Salvador. His father had connections in the U.S. and brought the family there to remove them from a harmful political situation. Gisele was born in Beirut, Lebanon, one of the oldest human settlements in the world. With the wars around the Mideast and a civil war raging within Lebanon, her father obtained sponsorship for the family from an uncle who lived in Los Angeles.

Although she arrived in the U.S. at 16 with no English, Gisele quickly caught up. While in college, a girlfriend, who was dating Sam's brother, introduced her to Sam and they soon became a couple. Sam started working in the film industry, doing hand-drawn special effects in animation. He spent ten years in the movie business, and Gisele became a preschool teacher.

As exciting as one might think it would be working for the biggest movie studios in Hollywood, Sam had always wanted his own business. The couple went off to Oregon to start a 7/11 franchise, but when Sam was called back to

Warner Brothers Studios in Los Angeles to work on the movie *Space Jam*, he and Gisele found themselves back in California. Not to be deterred from their vision, they made it back to Oregon, where they opened Plaza Latina supermarket, a Trader Joe's-like store that featured Hispanic foods.

After twelve years, working seven days a week was just too much for them, and Sam missed the Latin culture. Eventually, their oldest son was able to watch the business while Sam and Gisele explored possible south-of-the-border locations for a potential home. Costa Rica and Guatemala came under consideration, but Puerto Vallarta seemed the best bet. They stayed on the coast for two months and purchased a condo there. After a few years, though, it became clear that Puerto Vallarta just wasn't the right fit — they wanted something a little less urban.

Back in Portland, they'd already received their permanent visas. Now it was time to find the right place to settle. When Sam was invited Lakeside to run a pickleball clinic, they both enjoyed the area enough to begin looking for a home. A condo they liked became available and they put in an offer. Unfortunately, at the last minute the owner backed out.

It was back to Oregon again. One day, not long afterwards, the realtor they'd worked with called with the defining question, "If there's a nice house, but rundown, would you be interested in fixing it up?" She sent photos. They were intrigued. Seeing the photo was enough to inspire a trip to look at the house. They were sold, and so was the house.

The renovations took months, but while Gisele and Sam were ensconced in a nearby rental, he was able to get really involved with pickleball, a tennis-like sport that's played with a plastic ball and paddles. Having played with top professionals in the U.S., and with his organizational skills, he's helped the head coach make this game popular and accessible for both young and old.

Gisele and Sam still have a house and children in the U.S., but they now call Mexico home.

OLGA AND VSEVOLOD KAPLOUNENKO

When nineteen-year-old Olga married Vsevolod she began a perfect marriage with her soul mate. Their work, hers as an electrical engineer and his as a physicist, took them from Moscow to Sweden and then to the United States. However, it was lack of work, lack of health, and lack of finances that brought them to Mexico.

Expertise in superconductivity is not common; regardless, when Vsevolod lost his Silicon Valley job in 2009, he was unable to find other employment. Two years later he was diagnosed with early-onset Alzheimer's. Olga knew she'd soon have to leave her work to become her husband's caretaker. Adding his Alzheimer's to her Type 1 diabetes in the days before the Affordable Care Act meant health insurance was not an option, making health care in the U.S. out of reach.

Olga began doing research. In addition to good and affordable health care, she sought ease of immigration, low taxes, and proximity to the U.S. — their son was still in the San Francisco Bay Area. She entered "early retirement in Mexico" into a search engine and a questionnaire popped up. After filling in all her needs and desires, only one place met them all—Lake Chapala.

Then the next level of searching brought her to the *Focus on Mexico* site. She and Vsevolod signed up for the program and came to check out the area. After one day of walking around the area, Olga felt the peace she'd been needing to help her deal with the family stress. She made her decision.

The next two months were a whirlwind. Olga knew she had to act quickly. She got their immigration papers in order in just three days, obtaining permanent visas. Working with a realtor, she found a lot on the west side and a contractor who'd build a house in two months. During that time, she and her husband flew back to the Bay Area to sell their house and just about everything in it. She shipped her books, DVDs, television, kitchen items, guitar, and piano. Selling their home enabled them to buy a house here and still have savings. Too young to collect social security, their savings and money from a 401K kept them going.

While at first Olga was able to care for Vsevolod, she eventually realized they would both be better off moving him into a wonderful nursing home in San Juan Cosalá. She also knew that in order to deal with the stress and depression resulting from his deterioration, it would be best for her to get involved in other activities, and she easily discovered many opportunities.

Going to the monthly dinner for *Focus on Mexico* alumni she found some support, and eventually met a man who started as a compassionate friend, but developed into someone who'd be there for the best and the worst times. Typically a very social person, Olga continued to engage in other activities. She joined *Los Cantantes del Lago*, performed in *Thrill the World* and *Lip Sync*, acted in a few Little Theater productions, and started taking Zumba and tap classes. She's now teaching both.

She plans to stay in Mexico, not just because she can't afford to return to the states, but because her life here has become so fulfilling. She says, "Moving here is one of the best decisions I made in my life."

CHERIE SIBLEY WASYLIW

While many find their "here" in one of the villages around Lake Chapala, Mexico has numerous locations that seem to say "you're home now" to those who visit. When Cherie attended a convention in Puerto Vallarta back in 1992, it took only 24 hours for her to know she'd be living there. Upon her return to the states, she made the declaration to friends and family.

Over the course of the next four years, she returned to the area three or four times a year but had no specific plan. Then a number of things aligned that made the move doable. She and her husband divorced. The Internet made it possible for her to continue her marketing business online, and she began dating a man who expressed his interest in moving to Mexico.

They gave themselves one year. In that time, Cherie was on the go. She came down and found a house to rent outside of Puerta Vallarta, sold or gave away most of her belongings, and got her paperwork together. She and her friend made the drive to Puerto Vallarta with a dog and two cats in a covered pick-up, pulling a trailer. Her friend left after only one month, and though the rental agent was the only person Cherie knew, she always believed that "the universe provides." Sure enough, people stepped up and assisted with friendship and support.

Cherie made four promises to herself: learn to speak Spanish, return to the fine arts, learn to cook authentic Mexican food, and buy a house. With six months of intensive language classes she became fluent in Spanish. She began a four-year study of painting with an established artist and improved so much she was able to start her own small school teaching painting to adults. In addition, several galleries picked up her work—Galleria Dante, Galería Pacífico, and Galería Demetro.

Buying a house was a bigger challenge for Cherie since she'd moved down with no money, but some things are just meant to be. She knew that if she was in the real estate industry she would gain exposure to more possibilities. As it happened, the woman that had found her the rental wanted a website for her business and Cherie's background in graphic design and marketing made her an obvious choice. One thing led to another and she was able to work with them selling real estate.

After a while, she realized she could break away and have her own business, but needed to form a corporation, lease a property, and get rolling. Synchronistically, a couple she'd helped to settle in to a property after renting from the agency she'd been working for called her one day asking how they could help her, since she had helped them so much. After telling them her ideas they decided to bankroll her business for the first two years.

Then she found a house from a man who let her make payments over time. Bit by bit, over seventeen years, she reliably paid until she had full ownership. Eventually she sold her business to a Mexican man and rented rooms in her house to him and his employees. You might say things came together in a full circle.

Even living in Puerta Vallarta had a full circle element. Cherie had grown up in the deep woods on 75 acres in rural Southern Louisiana. She appreciated the area's simpler life and loved being surrounded by nature.

The arts were responsible for another circle. In 2007

Cherie hosted an art exhibition in her home. A friend brought along a man to introduce to Cherie. They began dating and after three years, they married.

Cherie says, "Art has walked beside me my whole life. I face all the challenges life throws at me, confident that it will continue to sustain me." Art came with her to Mexico and grew and evolved as she did. "I am a learning junkie....as long as me and my work are evolving, life will sustain me."

Puerto Vallarta, Jalisco, Mexico

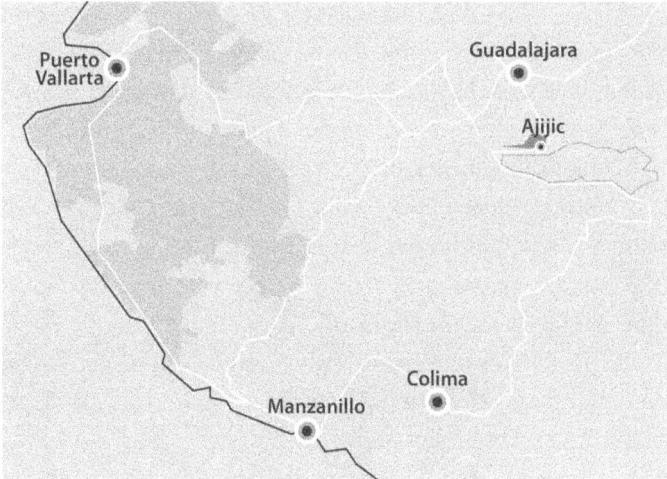

Puerto Vallarta is on the Pacific Ocean's Bahia de Banderas, approximately 190 miles from Guadalajara in the State of Jalisco. It's known for its beaches, night life and art. Along with its famous beaches, the area also lays claim to a nearby jungle environment that is noted for its density as well as its lush appearance. The region that Puerto Vallarta calls home boasts some of the most fascinating biodiversity of any in North America.

CYNTHIA AND BOB CAYWOOD

Near Barra de Navidad, slightly north of Manzanillo, lies the beachside village Villa Obregon. Flying back to the states from one of our yearly visits to Manzanillo my husband Thomas and I were fortunate to have seats on a sparsely populated plane a few rows from a woman who obviously shared the same love of silver jewelry as I do—Cynthia Caywood. We struck up a conversation that lasted the entire four hours. The flight attendant joined our chat whenever she had a moment, with the excuse of refilling our wine glasses. We were having such a grand time that other women from back in the plane drifted up to join our little group.

Back in California, Cindy and I continued our relationship with random phone calls. Thomas and I also made a point to visit Cindy and Bob at their home near Barra de Navidad — 45 minutes from our place in Manzanillo — during a few of our next visits.

Cynthia was born in Washington and raised in Alaska, where she and Bob met. Their marriage in 1973 precipitated their subsequent move to Mexico. After marrying, they traveled to Baja, spending four months on the sunny beaches. Both agreed the life there was what they wanted for themselves once they retired. Over the years they returned to Baja again and again, but during that time the area changed. It was becoming increasingly upscale. Baja no longer appealed to them, but with Mexico as their goal, they began looking to the mainland for a destination.

Bob found Cuastecomates on VRBO, the vacation

rental site. They came down for two weeks, rented a car and drove all around the area looking at various locations. By 2010 both Bob and Cindy were retired and ready to move. Cindy had met a woman in the small village of Jaluco who suggested they check it out as an option.

Back in the states, they sold their house, had a few garage sales, and bought an enclosed trailer that they loaded with Cindy's mosaic art supplies, a few pieces of furniture, clothes, and their dog. The two free spirits had no plan, no rental. They just drove down and showed up. In a few days they found a place to rent and moved in. One day, they met a young man who told them about a great house in Marabasco, less than an hour inland, nearer to Manzanillo, and off they went. Two years later, Bob and Cindy decided to move again.

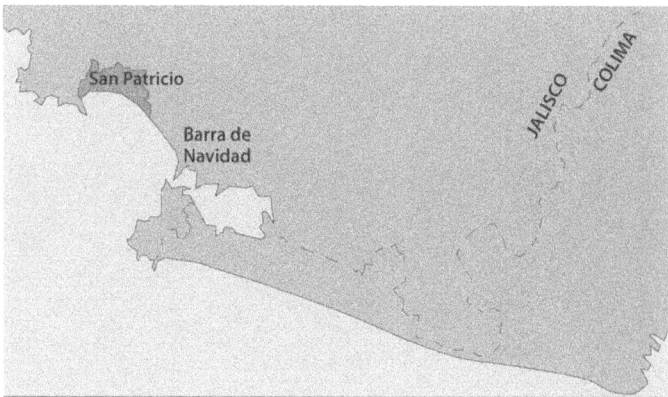

This time it was to Villa Obregon, where Cindy has a studio and creates marvelous mosaic art, sometimes on commission, while Bob makes rosaries which he gives to friends. They love the peaceful small town and the people there. Though neither are fluent in Spanish, 80% of their friends are local Mexicans.

While Cindy flies back to the states periodically to see family, Bob has never been back. He rides his bike five times a day, makes jewelry, and hangs out with Cindy and their three dogs. What a life.

CHAPTER 4

THE STORY OF TRANSITION

You've read just thirteen of the numerous life-changing stories to be found.

We all have a story to tell. In fact, we each have many stories. The stories we tell about our lives—who we are, what we believe—define us. "Who are you?" is a question that cannot be answered simply by stating your name. Some of us become who we were conditioned to be. Others are led by curiosity and a sense of adventure. The interest in what else is out there, and the question of what else is possible, can be catalysts for a life transition.

"Transitions or turning points, even when positive, signify moving toward something new and possibly unfamiliar. What *was* may be incorporated and used as a springboard toward the new, or it may be left behind. Those aspects of change — the unknown ahead, and the loss of what was — can make the experience of change difficult. We often undergo a period of feeling out of balance until we can accustom ourselves to the differences. Even when the life change is a sought-after improvement like a new home, it is not uncommon to find that the first months bring the confusion and insecurity of adjusting to a new role, in a new environment, and new responsibilities. ... Discovering ways to incorporate and adjust to the newness can be a demanding challenge. It entails finding an equilibrium between the outer expression of the change and our inner relationship to it."[1]

Cognitive dissonance often occurs when someone moves to a county that has different customs, traditions, and language than those they were accustomed to and considered normal, even right. When there is an inconsistency in behaviors and beliefs, it's likely a person will experience discomfort.

Not everyone is willing, or even able, to change their beliefs, attitudes, and behaviors. It's not uncommon to hear newcomers complain about the *mañana* attitude that seems prevalent here.

The incorporation stage of a rite of passage involves identifying oneself in a new and different way. Some people shed beliefs as easily as a snake sheds its skin to allow further growth. Others attempt to impose their previous beliefs and customs onto the new culture. Yet, as Neale Donald Walsch said, "Life begins at the end of your comfort zone."

Talking to many expats beyond those you've read about here, I've learned the incorporation stage may be a bit stressful, but undeniably worthwhile. For those who hadn't previously spent much time south of the border, or had come from countries with very different values, beliefs, and lifestyle, culture shock may initially create discomfort. There may be disorientation in adapting to the lack of language skills while adjusting to different customs. Learning to do banking, figuring out the telephone, driving rules, the many and frequent holidays, and the relaxed sense of time can be confounding. These things take getting used to.

Some expats live in a kind of bubble, spending time mainly with the large English-speaking community, shopping at the higher-end stores that have familiar products, and doing things that would more or less replicate what was in their comfort zone.

However, for many, immersion into a new culture is part of their goal in making the transition. It's not just the climate, lower cost of living, and excellent health care that people promote as reasons for retiring to Mexico. When you leave behind family and friends, and maybe work, you have the freedom to explore what is really meaningful for you. It's easy to find others who are doing or have done the same. New friends are easy to make, especially since "old friends" and family are elsewhere. Activities that were always a "someday" intention become a regular part of life.

The expats here are mostly experiencing what British historian Peter Laslett called the Third Age. These years, up to about age 80, fall into a period of personal achievement and fulfillment. Health and cognitive abilities still enable residents to enjoy a wide diversity of travel, sports, arts, and culture.

In her book, *The Second Half of Life: Opening the Eight Gates of Wisdom*[2], Angeles Arrien writes, "From age fifty onward, we know that there will be four broad frontiers to face:

- Retirement: from what to what?
- The possibility of becoming a mentor, steward, or grandparent.
- Coping with the natural challenges of maintaining the health of an aging body.

- Mortality: losing our loved ones, and the inevitability of our own death.

According to data from *World Population Prospects: the 2017 Revision*, the number of older persons — those aged 60 years or over — is expected to more than double by 2050 and to more than triple by 2100, rising from 962 million globally in 2017 to 2.1 billion in 2050 and 3.1 billion in 2100. Globally, the population aged 60 or over is growing faster than all younger age groups.[3]

LEVELS AND TRENDS IN POPULATION AGING

In 2017, there were an estimated 962 million people aged 60 or over in the world, comprising 13% of the global population. The population aged 60 or above is growing at a rate of about 3% per year... By 2050 all regions of the world except Africa will have nearly a quarter or more of their populations at ages 60 and above. The number of older persons in the world is projected to be 1.4 billion in 2030, 2.1 billion in 2050, and could rise to 3.1 billion in 2100.

Globally, the number of persons aged 80 or over is projected to triple by 2050, from 137 million in 2017 to 425 million in 2050. By 2100 it is expected to increase to 909 million, nearly seven times its value in 2017.[4]

The last census in Mexico was taken in 2010. At that time, the popular village of Ajijic had about 10,500 residents. Of course, not all were expats. In 2018, the best research is still vague as to the number of expats Lakeside, but with my best calculations of the estimated numbers I come up with about 24,000. Of these, the majority would easily be recognized as past or quickly approaching age 60.

Leaving behind one's youth and accepting the transition

to being an elder, whatever that may look like, will be the new "new thing."

IT REALLY DOES SEEM TO BE A SMALL WORLD

As I said in the introduction, a rite of passage follows the stages of a ritual. Creating a ritual to support or celebrate any passage can make it more meaningful. The following is an ongoing ritual I created for incorporating my move.

When we left the San Francisco Bay Area, I did not plan to return to California. In the forty years I'd lived in the area I developed relationships with friends, neighbors, colleagues, and students, many of whom had become very important to me. Once we settled into our new home in Mexico I realized that, while I had no desire to return to the states, I did value the relationships I had there and wanted to maintain them if I could.

In *The Art of Ritual*, Renee Beck and I write about clarifying the intention. "Why are you thinking about doing (this)? What has happened that...inspires you? What do you want it to accomplish? Who will this ritual affect?"

I decided to write a monthly newsletter describing our new life, adding the interesting and unusual experiences, the activities we participated in, and stories and images about the area and its customs.

As I planned how I'd go about this, I found a few emotional issues arose — excitement about the idea and doubt that recipients would be interested in reading about our monthly lives. I leaned toward excitement. I realized opening an email draft and listing interesting things as they occurred would also help me remember and re-experience the wonders of our new lives.

In the preparation stage, I added photos I'd taken or links I'd found that would enhance my descriptions.

Month's end was the time for execution. I ordered the events and turned them into an upbeat, personal story. When I was satisfied with the story, I clicked Bcc and added names of people I hoped would want to hear from me. I also encouraged a response and even a suggestion to visit.

Evaluating this process was enlightening. I heard back from people I hadn't expected to hear from and didn't from those I thought would respond. At one point I realized that saving the monthly emails gave me a journal of our time here. Re-reading the first year has evoked such good memories that otherwise might have been lost. It has helped me realize how I've integrated into my new life "here."

"You have brains in your head. You have feet in your shoes. You can steer yourself in any direction you choose. You're on your own. And you know what you know. And you are the one who'll decide where to go."— Dr. Seuss, "Oh the Places You'll Go"

RESOURCES

Moving to another country begins with a dream and is followed by an intention. While desire and intent can be strong motivators, research is a necessary component of a successful move.

Some people do all their research online exploring sites like LiveandInvestOverseas.com, which shares information on the top destinations for retirement worldwide.

YouTube features over 150 videos made by Jerry Brown and his wife Lori. Having traveled to over 35 countries, they focus on Southeast Asia and Mexico, offering a wealth of information that helps people planning to retire.

Others find the information they seek in books like *Moving to Mexico's Lake Chapala*, by Lisa L. Jorgensen. Lisa's guidebook covers immigration, legal basics, medical care, banking, and many incidentals.

Then there are those who enroll in programs that provide a classroom kind of experience. One of these, the *Focus on Mexico* program, originally founded by Ray and Marie Dwyer-Bullock back in 1995, provided the material and support for several of the individuals and couples inter-viewed in this book. In the six-day program held at a local Lakeside hotel, local professionals gave talks in their areas of expertise. These were interspersed with experiences that included day trips, restaurants, and a "behind the walls" tour.

No matter how much research you do, there will always be more questions and new challenges. Here are some of the basics:

Research and Planning Details

- Type, size of desired location
- Expat community
- Shopping
- Restaurants
- Transportation options
- Health care
- Immigration
- Driving
- Safety and security
- Religious/spiritual community
- Communications

Making the Move

- Visas
- Currency/banking
- Renting vs buying
- Mode of transition
- What to leave (sell, store, donate)
- What to bring and how
- Pets

- Change of address
- Voting
- Insurance

APPENDIX: TALES FROM MEXICO

SYDNEY AND THOMAS

I'd mentioned that one of the ways I incorporated into our new life here was to document it each month. I added things that were new and interesting to me into a document throughout the month, and at the end of the month wrote up a few paragraphs. Here are a few examples

We moved to Mexico in September of 2017, but as of March 1st, 2018 we have our own home. Moving from the rental was way more complicated and more work than we imagined. Planning helped, but there were so many unknowns that flexibility was imperative.

We packed and moved room by room, beginning with the most necessary rooms —kitchen and bedroom. Big surprise when we got to the new kitchen. The cabinets were appalling. Dark dusty wood, or should I say particle board, with shelves that ranged from okay to deteriorating. Flexibility and emergency thinking gave us a temporary fix. Three girlfriends with a roll of oil cloth working over the course of an entire day gave us a functional kitchen.

First day of Summer, June 21st. It seems we have officially entered the rainy season. It is now early afternoon and half the sky is bright blue with rays of sun bringing the temperature to the low 70's. But just slightly over to the side, there are large, fluffy cumulus clouds in gorgeous formations. Then a bit further on is the darkening sky. There's no telling when an enormous, and possibly brief cloudburst will occur. Generally, the rains come at night and early morning. Funny that you rarely see anyone using an umbrella to shield from rain, but women frequently use them to carry shade on hot sunny days.

Well this past month has really tested my skills in "adulting." I've had to deal with the DMV, Social Security, starting the renewal process on our visas, getting our house fumigated, renewing the car insurance, filling in our "end of life papers," in addition to the daily things we all deal with. I did it. Yay for me. I accept your virtual pats on the back. On the more pleasant side, the rains, often accompanied by rolling thunder and incredible lightning shows, have turned the mountains green and lush. The fields and roadsides are bursting with grasses and various plants. Last week, walking up the road with Mister Higgins (my dog), we passed a usually empty field that now featured three grazing horses, eight cows, a goat, and a few chickens. Where did they come from? While it's not unusual to see cows or horses sauntering down the road seemingly without a destination in mind, having them just appear in the fields is a new experience for me.

One of the biggest lessons I've learned is flexibility. Many of us have adopted the motto, "It is what it is." The other day, we had a bunch of CFE (Federal Electricity Commission) workers in the *fraccionamiento* (a kind of residential subdivision) yesterday digging holes to replace the old and damaged utility poles. While digging they managed to break one or more of our underground water pipes.

When the workers left there was a slow leak, but by 11 p.m. a neighbor walking his dog heard water running, and miraculously, just in the nick of time. The water storage for the entire neighborhood is in a big tank on the street above us that is gated and locked at 9 p.m. Two neighbors managed to shut off the upper and lower valves. Of course, the water distribution system to the frac was down all day while the pipe was being repaired.

Arts and culture abound. My intention is to participate in something in some way every week. November begins with what might be the most important holiday of the year — *Dia de los Muertos*. Altars (*ofrendas*) are created at Plazas all over Mexico, as well as in front of and within shops and homes. On this day, families welcome their deceased relatives back from the spirit world to the realm of the living. I visited a good-sized cementario on the West side of Ajijic. Vendors sold candles, flowers, food and drink outside the gate. Inside was another world. Entire families sat or even reclined on blankets in the square gravesites. People cleared the graves of debris, brought elaborate decorations and set out foods, drinks and various items to welcome their departed. Of course, the living enjoyed much more of the comestibles than the spirits. Music, folk dance, and theater went on for hours on a back patio. It was common to see men, women and children dressed as *Catrinas*, or with skull-painted faces.

The following week we had the three-day *Feria Maestros del Arte*. This annual event hosts 85 of the best folk artisans from around the country. The *Feria* was created to offer indigenous artists a venue to sell their work. Local families host the artists, who bring an array of wonderful work that includes *alebrijes* (painted wood

fantasy animals), ceramics, textiles, clothing, copper, furniture, jewelry and more.

The Lake Chapala Society (LCS) *is the go-to place for
people who've moved to the area.* They offer movies, classes,
a huge English library, events, and bus trips. Recently, a
good-sized group of us visited *Zoologico y Safari Guadalajara*, or in other words, the Guadalajara Zoo. This is an
enormous and beautiful park that's home to all manner of
animals, birds, and sea life. One highlight was the tram that
travels over the giraffe encloser. We were given handfuls of
chopped vegetables and the friendly giraffes came up to the
cars and ate right from our hands. It was an amazing
experience.

NOTES

INTRODUCTION

1. Beck, Renee and Metrick, Sydney. *The Art of Ritual*

1. WHAT A COINCIDENCE

1. http://qroo.us/2018/11/09/why-we-chose-to-retire-in-mexico-instead-of-the-u-s/
2. https://www.expatsinmexico.com/how-many-expats-live-in-mexico/
3. U.S. State Department, INEGI, CONAPO, INM, Forbes, El Financiero
4. https://www.theyucatantimes.com/2017/09/have-you-ever-wondered-how-many-expats-live-in-mexico/
5. https://mexiconewsdaily.com/opinion/10000-baby-boomers-retire-every-day/?utm_source=Mexico+News+Today&utm_campaign=2016606edf-MNT+jan23-2019&utm_medium=email&utm_term=0_f1536a3787-2016606edf-349536049

3. "RETIRING" TO MEXICO

1. http://www.thirdagecenter.com/whatisthirdage.htm

4. THE STORY OF TRANSITION

1. Beck, Renee and Metrick, Sydney. *The Art of Ritual* p. 5
2. Published March 1st 2006 by Sounds True (first published 1998). Original Title: *The Second Half of Life: Opening the Eight Gates of Wisdom* (ISBN 9781591792529)
3. https://esa.un.org/unpd/wpp/Publications/Files/WPP2017_Key-Findings.pdf
4. http://www.un.org/en/sections/issues-depth/ageing/

www.ingramcontent.com/pod-product-compliance
Lightning Source LLC
Chambersburg PA
CBHW031152090426
42738CB00008B/1306